Dedicated to Cookie

The Maryland Use of Force Handbook is written for informational purposes and is not intended to serve as legal advice or to form an attorney-client relationship between the authors, COHEN | HARRIS LLC, and the reader.

FOREWORD BY MARK W. PENNAK

"[T]he Second and Fourteenth Amendments protect an individual's right to carry a handgun for self-defense outside the home." So held the United States Supreme Court in *NYSRPA v. Bruen*, 597 U.S. 1, 10 (2022). Prior to that decision, Maryland was one of the few States that effectively denied that right by requiring law-abiding Marylanders to obtain a "wear and carry" permit, the issuance of which was conditioned on a showing of a special need ("a good and substantial reason") for self-protection. To get an unrestricted permit, the applicant essentially had to be a judge, a prosecutor, a criminal defense attorney or a person with a verified Top-Secret security clearance. The Supreme Court put an end to that "special need" restriction with its decision in *Bruen*. As a result, Marylanders with carry permits have grown from approximately 30,000 individuals in 2022 to over 200,000 individuals in 2024 and that number grows every day, notwithstanding the rigorous and expensive training requirements imposed by Maryland. This book is a must-read for every Marylander who has a carry permit or is contemplating obtaining such a permit. But this book is equally valuable to people who merely wish to know the law of self-defense, whether that be in the home or elsewhere, with a firearm or otherwise.

Successful self-defense does not end by dealing with an imminent threat of death or serious bodily harm. "Stopping the threat" is, of course, the first necessity, but it is only the beginning. The next step is contending with the criminal justice system, and for that, people need this book. As then-Attorney General Robert Jackson told a room full of federal prosecutors in a speech in 1940, "[t]he prosecutor has more control over life, liberty, and reputation than any other person in America." With the ever-increasing number and complexity of criminal laws enacted by the State and federal governments, that is even more true today. You need a lawyer, and that right to counsel is guaranteed by the Sixth Amendment to the Constitution. As the Supreme Court realized long ago in *Gideon v. Wainwright*, 372 U.S. 335, 344-45 (1963), the right to a fair trial and due process "cannot be realized" if the criminal defendant "has to face his accusers without a lawyer to assist him." How and when to claim this right is central to this book (hint, early and at every stage of the proceedings). People accused of crime, including when they are arrested for exercising the right of self-defense, are wholly defenseless against the prosecutor without an experienced lawyer by their side. Non-lawyers (and many lawyers who do not practice criminal law) are ill-equipped to deal with the criminal justice system in Maryland. This highly readable book is written for that audience and is undoubtedly the best collection of information and accumulated wisdom I have seen on these subjects.

Mark W. Pennak is the President of Maryland Shall Issue, Inc., a Section 501(c)(4), non-profit, non-partisan Second Amendment advocacy organization. Mr. Pennak is a firearms instructor certified by the National Rifle Association and by the Maryland State Police and is a member of the Maryland and District of Columbia Bars. He has practiced law in the U.S. Supreme Court and in all the federal courts of appeals for nearly 50 years in private practice and as an attorney with the United States Department of Justice. He is counsel for plaintiffs in cases currently pending in State and federal courts.

INDEX

1.0 Introduction 1

2.0 Things some people are surprised to learn about the criminal justice system in Maryland 5

2.1. The criminal justice system prosecutes people charged with violent crimes 5

2.2. The State doesn't need much evidence to charge you with a crime 6

2.3. There is no magic motion your lawyer can file that makes your case go away 7

2.4. Your right to a speedy trial doesn't mean today or tomorrow 9

2.5. Overall, the criminal justice system doesn't reward people for accepting responsibility 10

2.6. Being presumed innocent doesn't always feel like it 11

2.7. Best friends are not the best people to discuss your case with 12

3.0. The charges commonly filed in a Use of Force case 15

3.1. Murder in the First Degree 15

3.1a. Premeditation 17

3.1b. Preconceived Design 17

3.2. Murder in the Second Degree 18

3.3. Attempted Murder 19

3.4. Assault 20

3.5. Use of a Firearm in the Commission of a Felony or Crime of Violence 21

3.6. Reckless Endangerment 22

3.7. Manslaughter 22

4.0. Maryland's Legal Uses of Force.....................................25

4.1. Perfect Self-Defense 26

4.1a. Exceptions to the duty to retreat when using deadly force 27

4.1a(i). In your own home..27

4.1a(ii). Retreat was unsafe, or the route was unknown.....28

4.1a(iii). The victim of a robbery 28

4.1a(iv). Lawfully arresting the victim 30

4.1a(v). Concluding thoughts on the duty to retreat...........31

4.1b. Who must prove what in self-defense cases 31

4.2. Imperfect Self-Defense...32

4.3. Defense of Others...33

4.4. Defense of Habitation 34

4.4a. Trespassers 36

4.5. Defense of Property 37

5.0. You had to use force – Now what happens...................41

5.1. Assume that everything is recorded..............................41

5.1a. Surveillance Footage..41

5.1b. 911 Calls and Body Camera Footage...........................42

5.1c. Jail Calls 43

5.2. Speaking with the Police 44

5.2a. What can happen during your interactions with the Police 45

5.3. The media may be interested in your case 47

5.4. Do you charge the other party or not 47

5.4a. Peace and Protective Orders 48

5.5. What will happen as my case moves through the system 49

5.5a. Charging 50

5.5b. District and Circuit Courts 51

5.5b(i). District Court 52

5.5b(ii). Circuit Court 52

5.5c. Preliminary Hearings and Grand Juries 52

5.5d. Arraignment and Initial Appearances 53

5.5e. Pretrial Motions 54

5.5f. Trial 54

5.5f(i). Opening statement from the State's Attorney and witnesses 56

5.5f(ii). Putting on your case 56

5.4f(iii). Testifying at trial 57

6.0. Concluding words 63

Notes 64

1.0 Introduction

Roland S. Harris, IV and Martin E. Cohen are the senior partners of COHEN | HARRIS LLC, a law firm formed in 2017 to protect the rights of the people. We each have over 18 years of experience fighting for the rights of individuals in criminal defense cases as well as civil rights cases, including but not limited to 2nd Amendment issues. It has been said that COHEN | HARRIS LLC represents "both sides of the gun" because we represent individuals in cases ranging from the denial of 2nd Amendment Rights to victims of violent crimes, to people charged with Murder.

The purpose of this book is to give you, the reader, some insight into Maryland's use of force laws from the lawyer's perspective. It is impossible to crunch 36 years of experience into any book, but we are going to try. Maryland lawyers see the use of force a little differently from the rest of the world. Anywhere in the world if we were to stop a random person and ask them whether people should be able to defend themselves "if they feel that their safety is at risk, or their life was in danger" most people would respond by saying a resounding "hell yeah". But that is not how the court system works. Every state has its own definitions of legal uses of force and Maryland is no exception. When using force in Maryland one needs to think "would the courts in Maryland give me permission to scare or hurt someone in this situation". That is how Maryland lawyers are taught to think about your case, within the specific framework established by our court system.

Use of force cases hinge on the establishment of, or by negating, very specific facts, or pieces of evidence. By understanding what your lawyer is looking for, you will be able to give them the necessary information in a timely manner to help you win your case and, hopefully, keep your wits about you through the process. Keeping a level head will help you make legally sound decisions at the time of the conflict, during interactions with the police, and throughout the court process, should that occur.

As we all know, use of force situations are rapidly unfolding events. The more you understand the use of force laws of Maryland, the more it becomes incorporated into your actions during and following the event.

In the real world, no one expects everything to be perfect, but oddly it seems the court system does. If you do not meet the elements of self-defense, or the other forms of defense this book covers, you may find yourself convicted of several charges that will likely carry substantial jail time.

During this book, the term defendant will often be used. The fact that it is used should not be construed to mean someone who uses force will be accused of a crime or that the use of force is a crime. That term is used because often an attorney gets involved with a use of force case because there are either charges filed or likely pending. With that introduction, let's begin exploring the world of Maryland's use of force laws.

The Maryland Use of Force Handbook

Roland S. Harris, IV and Martin E. Cohen

2.0 Things some people are surprised to learn about the criminal justice system in Maryland

At times attorneys can find themselves having lengthy conversations with clients about things that the clients think are happening or should happen, when in fact those things are not something that occurs during a case in Maryland. Other states may do other things, but this is about Maryland.

2.1. The criminal justice system prosecutes people charged with violent crimes

You can't turn on your TV without a 24-hour news cycle telling you that violent offenders get set free all the time. It's intentionally scary and they report that nonsense because the news makes money by keeping you, the viewer, hooked to their channel. Human beings are inherently drawn to reports of violence and they play off that instinct.

The truth is, if you're charged with a violent crime, even Assault in the Second Degree, one of the least serious violent crimes we will discuss in this book, you face the possibility of being held without bail until your trial. The reality is the criminal justice system is less of a system and more like a casino. There is no checklist, where if you check off every box you can guarantee that you won't be prosecuted or convicted. Sometimes innocent people are convicted simply because they got the wrong prosecutor and the wrong judge or jury on the same day.

People accused of violent crimes go free at higher rates because a significant amount of violent crime is committed against other violent people.[1] Violent people cross paths,

---

[1] Reichert, Jessica MS and Mason, Maryann, PHD, Illinois Criminal Justice Information Authority, June 10, 2023 "Victim Offender Overlap: Firearm Homicide

commit acts of violence against each other, and then refuse to participate in the prosecution of a case. In the end, statistically, violent crimes are dismissed at a higher rate because, in many cases, the prosecution requires the participation of witnesses, and those witnesses refuse to participate. There are even times when witnesses that are necessary to prosecute a case want the charges dismissed against the defendant so the defendant can be released into the community where it's easier for the witnesses to carry out acts of retaliation and revenge.

The news reports statistics showing the rates of people charged with violent crimes getting released, without much, if any, exploration of the reasons for the dismissal of these cases. Based on this superficial reporting many people mistakenly think being charged with a violent crime is a walk in the park. Some people think "my case is a self-defense case, so obviously they will just dismiss it" while the court system treats them like they are going to prison for a long time.

2.2. The State doesn't need much evidence to charge you with a crime

Someone can simply say you did something, and you could be charged. There are very few provisions in the law that require a specific piece of evidence to prosecute. For example, many gun-related crimes do not require the state's attorney to produce a gun that was recovered from the defendant. The state's attorney can, in most cases, produce whatever evidence

---

Victims With And Without Criminal Records", https://icjia.illinois.gov/researchhub/articles/victim-offender-overlap-firearm-homicide-victims-with-and-without-criminal-records/

See also National Institute of Justice, March 11, 2021, "The Overlap Between Those Committing Offenses Who Are Also Victims: One Class Of Crime Victim Rarely Seeks Or Receives Available Services", https://nij.ojp.gov/topics/articles/overlap-between-those-committing-offenses-who-also-are-victims-one-class-crime

they think is sufficient to prove their case. So, things like videos, DNA, and fingerprints may be completely absent from a case but because a witness has pointed a finger at you, you could find yourself sitting in the defendant's chair.

2.3. There is no magic motion your lawyer can file that makes your case go away

Just to be clear, there are a slew of different motions that can be filed during your case that could get your case dismissed. For example, if you request the discovery in your case, the discovery being the evidence that the Maryland Rules require the state's attorney to disclose to the defense[2], and later, despite the defendant's request, the state's attorney refuses to turn over that evidence as the law requires, the defense could file a motion demanding the discovery or for the case to be dismissed. In that situation, a judge could rule that due to the failure of the state's attorney to produce the discovery the court is going to dismiss the case. Another example is when a trial is postponed due to the state's attorney and the defense makes a motion arguing that the defendant's right to a speedy trial has been violated. In that situation as well, a judge could rule that the defense is correct and dismiss the charges as a sanction against the state for violating the defendant's right to speedy trial.

But what can't a lawyer do? In Maryland, a lawyer can't file a motion based on the legal premise that "this is a self-defense case" or "this case is crap". There is no motion for "the witness is a liar", "their video is blurry" or "we have a witness that says this is what really happened". These issues come up in a lot of cases. Lawyers in Maryland do not have a court rule that allows

---

[2] See Maryland Rule 4-262 for the discovery rules in District Court and Maryland Rule 4-263 for Circuit Court.

them to just write that into a motion, file it with the court, and ask the court to dismiss the case.

In the State of Maryland, there are commonly only two occasions during which the court will determine whether there is sufficient evidence to proceed with the case. The first time is when you first get charged and the court commissioner determines whether there is probable cause to formally file charges against you. A court commissioner is not required to be a lawyer, and they make the initial determination for the criminal justice system in Maryland as to whether you can be charged with a crime.[3] The second time the court determines whether you can be charged with a crime is if you are charged with felony charges that are required to be prosecuted in the Circuit Court. For the felony charges to get to the Circuit Court, you are entitled to a public proceeding known as a preliminary hearing, which is held in front of a judge, or the matter may be indicted behind closed doors and without your presence, through the grand jury process. In both situations the question is whether probable cause exists to charge you for the felony counts and the felony counts are the only charges the court is considering.

Probable cause, in the context of preliminary hearings and grand jury appearances, means the state's attorney explains what evidence they have that a crime occurred and that the defendant committed it.[4] The evidence does not have to be strong, and the court is not required to consider the defendant's

---

[3] Maryland Courts and Judicial Proceedings § 2-607 Commissioners.
[4] *Freeman v.* State, 249 Md. App. 269, 301 (2021) noting that standards like "more likely than not" do not apply to the determination of whether probable cause exists. "'[P]robable cause' to justify an arrest means facts and circumstances within the officer's knowledge that are sufficient to warrant a prudent person, or one of reasonable caution, in believing, in the circumstances shown, that the suspect has committed . . . an offense." *Michigan v. DeFillippo*, 443 U.S. 31, 37 (1979).

use of self-defense during either proceeding. A lawyer for the defendant may argue self-defense at a preliminary hearing, and there may be times a judge is swayed by that argument, but there is no rule requiring the court to consider self-defense or any form of legal use of force defenses at a preliminary hearing.

Legal use of force in the State of Maryland is a defense that is asserted at trial. Unlike other states where a defendant might be able to have a pretrial hearing of some sort and move to dismiss the case on legal use of force grounds, in Maryland the legal justification is the defendant's defense for trial. That means that, depending on what a defendant elects during the trial, the defense could participate in the selection of a jury, give opening statements, cross-examine state's witnesses and confront their evidence, make mid-trial motions, present the defendant's evidence, make end of trial motions, get to closing arguments, and in closing statements the defense could then argue the legal use of force as their defense.

2.4. Your right to a speedy trial doesn't mean today or tomorrow

We all know about our right to a speedy trial, but some cases can take a year or more before they are resolved.[5] Different counties in Maryland handle criminal cases differently, but the general rule of thumb is the more serious the case, the longer it can be before trial. In some jurisdictions, a simple Assault in the Second Degree may only take a couple of weeks while in others

---

[5] See Maryland Rule 4-271 which mandates that a first trial date must be set within 180 days of the defendant's first appearance in the Circuit Court or the entry of their counsel into the Circuit Court case. This rule is commonly referred to as the *Hicks* rule or *Hicks* date after *State v. Hicks*, 285 Md. 310 (1979), the case from which the original rule was derived. If the court finds good cause to postpone a trial date beyond *Hicks* or the defendant waives *Hicks*, the court may be set a date beyond the 180 days. Once the court finds good cause to postpone the case beyond *Hicks* the rule no longer applies. See *Jules v. State*, 171 Md. App. 458, 479 (2006).

it takes months. The same is true for Murder cases where in some jurisdictions you may be setting trial dates a couple of months out while in others you are looking at the calendar for next year. Typically, the further out a trial date is, the less willing the court is to allow a postponement.

The result is that this process can take a substantial amount of time during which you are trying to live life. You could be in jail or held on home detention and restricted to your house the entire time.

2.5. Overall, the criminal justice system doesn't reward people for accepting responsibility

One of the most shocking things in the criminal justice system is seeing how the system does not generally support those who accept responsibility. We are all taught that if you do something, right or wrong, go to someone and tell them what you did and people are going to say you accepted responsibility and, by doing so, people will cut us a break. The criminal justice system, in large part, operates in a manner that is opposite of that premise.

In the criminal justice system, the people who confess to a crime and/or turn over the evidence that will be used against them – tend to get the worst treatment. The people who remain silent and refuse to turn anything over without a search warrant fare far better in the criminal justice system. People give statements to the police or other pieces of evidence that become cornerstones of the state's case, and they get demolished at trial. In Maryland, if you speak with the police, the state's attorney is not obligated to present your statement in court if it helps you. And, on the other hand, you may be prohibited from using your statement unless, in a rare circumstance, you can establish that your statement fits within one of a few limited exceptions.[6]

To add insult to injury, if a defendant pleads guilty in Maryland, they will usually have to ask the appellate courts for permission to appeal, which is often denied. Whereas if the defendant went to trial, they would have an automatic right to appeal their case and could raise any legally viable ground that occurred during their trial to overturn their conviction.[7]

This is a good reason to speak with an attorney immediately following a use of force situation and before providing anything to the police.

2.6. Being presumed innocent doesn't always feel like it

Starting with the bail review, the state's attorney is probably going to talk about you like you are already guilty, and sometimes even the judge will chime in with similar sentiments. It is not uncommon for the courts to ignore or even halt any discussion about the "victim" or the circumstances and instead use those factors to say you have a motive to do further harm to the so-called "victim". It can sound like they are hung up on the charging documents filed against you.

The same can happen with news reports. The news will report that an innocent person was gunned down when you know the "victim" is or was a scoundrel who forced you to act in self-defense. It can feel like everyone is talking to you as though you are already guilty. Don't be surprised when people talk in that manner. The main thing to keep in mind is that

---

[6] See Maryland Rule 5-801 through 806 for prohibitions and potential exceptions for admissibility.
[7] See Courts and Judicial Proceedings § 12-302(e)(2) Appeals not permitted, see also Maryland Rule 8-204 Application for leave to appeal.

those comments in no way mean that you will be convicted or that you are guilty of anything.

Often the state's attorney, the court, or the news are not able to take the time necessary to learn all the facts. They form opinions based on very little information and wait until the trial to change their minds. You must keep your chin up in those situations and stand strong.

2.7. Best friends are not the best people to discuss your case with

We all know what opinions are like. Everybody has friends they talk to about the events in their lives and when you are in gun communities such as hunting lodges and collectors' groups, a use of force case is a hot topic. You need to understand that when people find out that you have such a case, they WILL want to tell you about what happened in their friend's case or even worse, their cousin's - best friend's - uncle's case, and, based on this anecdotal knowledge, they WILL want to tell you how to handle your situation.

The problem with this is two-fold. First, there can be things that seem minor to your friends, so they don't tell you those parts or maybe they never knew those parts at all. They are telling you what they think is important and you are telling them what you think is important, but neither side is an attorney. Two lawyers discussing your case might have a totally different discussion about what's going on because what is important in the eyes of the law might be divergent from what non-lawyers think.

Secondly, you shouldn't talk to anybody about your case because you never really know who is ultimately going to get called as a witness, and how they're going to recount what it is that you said during your conversations. For the same reason, you need to be careful about what you post on social media. You should inform your lawyer about any communications that you have regarding your case.

3.0 The charges commonly filed in a legal use of force case

During this section, we are going to give you an overview of the most common charges someone could face where legal use of force was utilized. In these cases, state's attorneys can, and do, charge other crimes, but the purpose of this chapter is to educate you about the most common and very often the most serious charges.

3.1. Murder in the First Degree

In Maryland, a Murder in the First Degree is a deliberate, premeditated, and willful killing.[8] Murder in the First Degree carries a life sentence. That can be life with the possibility of parole or without. Our courts have a system called the Maryland Sentencing Guidelines that the state's attorney and the court can use to calculate a recommended sentence upon conviction.[9] With Murder in the First Degree, the guidelines are always life to life regardless of your criminal record.

A state's attorney could file a motion requesting that the court impose a sentence of life without parole.[10] Just because

---

[8] Maryland Criminal Law § 2-201 Murder in the First Degree. As one can see from a review of Maryland Criminal Law § 2-201 in its totality there are other forms of Murder in the First Degree, but this writing will focus on the one most likely to occur in the use of force case.

[9] See Maryland Criminal Procedure § 6-208 Sentencing Guidelines and Maryland Criminal Procedure § 6-216 Judicial Sentencing Guidelines, see also, Code of Maryland Regulations (COMAR) 14.22.01.01 - 17 General Regulations and 14.22.02.00 - 02 Criminal Offense and Seriousness Categories.

[10] See Maryland Criminal Law § 2-203 Murder in the first degree – Sentence of imprisonment for life without the possibility of parole and Maryland Criminal Law § 2-304 First Degree Murder – Sentencing procedure imprisonment for life without the possibility of parole. Note that Md. CL § 2-304(b) contains a provision giving a jury the power to determine whether life without parole should be imposed and the considerations the jury should make in coming to their conclusion. Maryland Criminal Law § 2-304(b) was "repealed by implication" and no longer has any effect per the ruling of the then Maryland Court of Appeals in *Bellard v. State*, 452 Md. 467 (2017), which held that Maryland Criminal Law § 2-304(a) endows the Court, and not the Jury, with the

you have been convicted of Murder in the First Degree doesn't automatically mean you get life without parole, the state's attorney must file a motion asking the court to impose it. If the motion is properly filed, the court will use its discretion as to whether it should grant the state's motion after hearing arguments from both the state's attorney and defense.

On a life sentence with parole, a person must serve 20 years before they're eligible for parole.[11] When someone goes up for their first parole hearing, after 20 years, it is highly unlikely that they will be paroled at their first hearing. Once a person has received a life with parole sentence, they are pretty much guaranteed to have to serve more than 20 years.

With almost any conviction, a judge can impose what is known as a split sentence, meaning they can give a portion of the sentence to be served immediately and the rest suspended, so you do not have to serve the suspended portion of the sentence unless you violate the terms the court imposes, and subsequently, the court orders a term of probation that follows the portion of the sentence you have to serve. The ability to split a sentence is a way many criminal cases are resolved. Although a judge can give a split sentence at the end of a trial, in Murder cases, split sentences are often part of a pre-trial plea offer but are far less common when someone is found guilty after a trial. If a split sentence is the outcome of your case, for violent crimes, a person must serve 50% of their jail sentence before they become eligible for parole. For example, if the judge says, "life suspending all but 50 years", the defendant must serve 25 years before they become eligible for parole. The advantage of a split sentence in a Murder case is that you have a release date, which

---

power to make the determination as to whether life without imprisonment should be imposed.
[11] Maryland Correctional Services § 7-301(d)(1)(ii) twenty years for offenses committed on or after October 1, 2021.

is a firm date on which your sentence will expire, the disadvantage is that it could push out your parole date as is the case of a life suspend all but 50 years outcome for a Murder in the First Degree conviction.

3.1 a. Premeditation

The form of Murder in the First Degree most relevant to use of force cases requires premeditation. Premeditation means that the defendant had sufficient time to consider the decision whether to kill and weigh the reasons for or against killing.[12] In some state's attorneys' minds, this is as short as the time it takes to pull a trigger. State's attorneys often argue that the first shot might not have been Murder. Maybe it was self-defense at first, but not the second shot and not the third shot. Now we have arrived at a point where you're using too much force, the threat is abated and you've had time to think about it. The state's attorney will argue that in the process of defending yourself, you went from acting in self-defense to being a murderer acting in the first degree.

3.1 b. Preconceived Design

In Maryland, we have a legal theory known as preconceived design. What that means is that you had a weapon in advance of the need to have it. So, if you have a concealed carry permit it makes sense why you have a firearm but if you're in a situation where you do not have a concealed carry permit, and you have a firearm in advance of the threat, the law considers that to be a preconceived design.[13]

In that situation, the state's attorney can use preconceived design to jam you up in two ways:

---

[12] *Wiley v. State*, 328 Md. 126, 138 (1992).
[13] *State v. Crawford*, 308 Md. 683 (1987).

1. They argue that you had the weapon because you were planning to have a confrontation, and/or;

2. They argue that even if you win your use of force claim you are still guilty of possessing the firearm or other weapon illegally and therefore are subject to penalties for carrying the item.

This is a good reason to have a Maryland Wear Carry permit to prevent this argument and because jurors and judges look more favorably on someone who uses weapons they legally possess.[14]

3.2. Murder in the Second Degree

Murder in the First Degree may be the only charge on an indictment.[15] You will look at the indictment and it will say Murder in the First Degree but, in Maryland, that can also mean you are charged with Murder in the Second Degree. The reason is because Murder in the Second Degree is the same as Murder in the First Degree, but in the form that is most prosecuted in legal use of force cases Murder in the Second Degree does not require premeditation. The courts refer to this type of charge as a "lesser included". There are times when an indictment will have Murder in the Second Degree listed as a charge, but it is not required if there is also a charge of Murder in the First Degree.[16]

---

[14] See Maryland Public Safety § 5-306 for qualifications to obtain a wear carry permit in Maryland.

[15] *Middleton v. State*, 238 Md. App. 295, 309 (2018).

[16] In a case where Murder in the Second Degree is pursued by the state as a lesser included of a Murder in the First charge for a single victim a defendant cannot be convicted of both counts. Both can appear on a verdict sheet given to a jury and used for documenting their verdict, but the jury should be instructed to skip Murder in the Second if the defendant is convicted of Murder in the First and only decide Murder in the Second if the verdict on Murder in the First is not guilty.

State's attorneys love falling back on this charge because they don't have to argue about premeditation. Sometimes jurors think they're doing the defendant a favor by not convicting them of Murder in the First Degree for a case that they think falls outside of a form of legal use of force, except Murder in the Second Degree carries a 40 year maximum penalty and as with other violent charges in Maryland, the defendant will have to serve 50% of the sentence before they are eligible for parole.

3.3. Attempted Murder

Attempted Murder is a sticky charge. Attempted Murder in the First Degree carries the same maximum penalty as Murder in the First and Attempted Murder in the Second Degree carries 30 years. For an attempted crime, all the State's Attorney is required to prove is that "a substantial step beyond mere preparation" was taken in the commission of the charge alleged, for the purposes of this discussion Murder, and that the defendant had the apparent ability to commit the crime.[17] For example, you could find yourself charged with Attempted Murder in the First Degree and facing a life sentence for a shot or the swing of a weapon that didn't hit anything. Here at COHEN|HARRIS we refer to crimes that are charged as attempts as being sticky because the term "substantial step beyond preparation" is vague and the state's attorney is given tremendous leeway to charge crimes like Attempted Murder in situations where less serious charges would have been more appropriate. In terms of sentencing, the only advantage of Attempted Murder in the First Degree is that you cannot get life without parole for Attempted Murder in the First Degree and the maximum penalty is 30 years for Attempted Murder in the

---

[17] See Maryland Criminal Law § 2-205 for Attempt to commit Murder in the First Degree and § 2-206 for Attempt to commit Murder in the Second Degree. See also Maryland Pattern Jury Instruction 4:17.13 Attempted First and Second Degree Murder.

Second Degree.

3.4. Assault

As with Murder, there are two levels of Assault with different sentences. Assault in the Second Degree is a misdemeanor that carries a 10-year maximum sentence. Assault in the Second Degree comes in three forms:

1. Attempting to touch someone without their permission;

2. Touching someone without their permission; or

3. Putting a person in fear of being touched without their permission.[18]

Then there is Assault in the First Degree which is a felony and carries a 25-year maximum sentence. There are three ways for the state's attorney to prove Assault in the First Degree:

1. They prove the defendant intentionally caused or attempted to cause serious physical injury to another;

2. That the defendant committed an Assault using a firearm; or

3. That the defendant committed an Assault by intentionally strangling another person.[19]

Note that in the first two ways of proving Assault in the First Degree, there is no requirement that anyone is touched at all. The form of Assault in the First Degree that entails using a firearm during an Assault looks exactly the Use of a Firearm in the Commission of a Crime of Violence, a crime we will discuss in the following section because both crimes punish the same

---

[18] See Maryland Pattern Jury Instruction Cr 4:01 Second Degree Assault.
[19] Maryland Criminal Law § 3-202 Assault in the First Degree.

behavior. You will see how the Use of a Firearm and Assault in the First Degree together, do nothing but double-up the penalty.

3.5. Use of a Firearm in the commission of a Felony or Crime of Violence

This is one of the stickiest and scariest charges of them all. The state's attorney simply needs to prove that the defendant committed a felony or crime of violence and that a firearm was used during the commission of that offense.[20] The firearm does not even need to be functioning or what the courts call "operable".[21] Use does not mean firing a weapon, simply displaying the firearm in the commission of an Assault is enough to get someone convicted of this charge.

Use of a Firearm in the Commission of a Felony or Crime of Violence carries a maximum penalty of 20 years and a mandatory minimum of 5 years without parole. Once convicted of this charge a person must serve at least 5 years in prison without any reductions to their sentence.

There are cases where judges don't necessarily like sentencing under this law. Situations arise where the case itself does not warrant 5 years in jail, but because of this nonsensical law the judge has no choice but to impose this sentence. Regardless of how much of a model inmate someone is, no matter how many programs they do, or jobs they work, they are going to be in jail for 5 years if convicted.

In addition to the harsh penalty, this law covers a slew of crimes labeled as crimes of violence, including Assault in the Second Degree, which as we discussed earlier, doesn't require a

---

[20] See Maryland Criminal Law § 4-204 Use of a firearm in commission of crime.
[21] See Maryland Pattern Jury Instruction 4:35.4B – "A firearm is a weapon that fires, is designed to fire, or may be readily converted to fire a projectile by the action of an explosive or the frame or receiver of such a weapon."

person to be touched at all.[22] Also, there are times when a jury may decide to acquit a defendant of the more serious sounding crimes but decide to convict of lesser charges thinking they are doing justice without realizing that a conviction for Assault in the First Degree and Use of a Firearm in the Commission of a Crime of Violence exposes the person to 45 years altogether and a mandatory minimum of 5 years in prison.

3.6. Reckless Endangerment

Reckless Endangerment carries a 5-year maximum penalty, and the state's attorney just has to prove that the defendant acted recklessly, in a manner a reasonable person would not have or the defendant discharged a firearm from a motor vehicle and that the reckless act created a substantial risk of serious bodily harm to another person.[23]

For this charge, it is not uncommon for someone to receive probation and to not have to serve jail time if they are compliant with the terms of their probation. Also, Reckless Endangerment is a misdemeanor so there is another bonus. Take note that although this seems like a much better outcome compared to Murder or Use of Firearm charges, a conviction for Reckless Endangerment can result in a lifetime ban from the possession of firearms, so it is important to discuss alternative methods of sentencing and expungement options with your attorney.[24]

3.7. Manslaughter

Manslaughter can be charged as an offense, meaning it is listed as a count on your charging documents, or Voluntary Manslaughter can be the result of a verdict involving the

---

[22] See Maryland Public Safety 5-101(c) for the list of crimes of violence violative of Maryland Criminal Law § 4-204.
[23] Maryland Criminal Law § 3-204.
[24] Maryland Criminal Procedure § 6-220(c)(1) is a form of probation before judgement available in Maryland that does not impose a guilty finding during the plea process and is intended to prevent issues with federal law.

Imperfect Defense of Self, Others or Habitation as will be explained later in section 4.2 of this book. This section will discuss when a person is charged with Manslaughter as an offense. Manslaughter as an offense comes in two different forms:

1. Voluntary Manslaughter is an "intentional homicide, done in a sudden heat of passion, caused by adequate provocation, before there has been a reasonable opportunity for the passion to cool".

2. Involuntary Manslaughter is an "unintentional killing done without malice, by doing some unlawful act endangering life, or negligently doing some act lawful in itself, or by the negligent omission to perform a legal duty"[25]

Manslaughter is punishable by up to 10 years imprisonment.[26] It is rare that this charge shows on charging documents, and is more likely to come into play at a trial as a result of it being a charge included in short form indictments used in Maryland to charge Murder.[27] It is important that you discuss this confusing topic with your attorney if you are charged with either Murder or Attempted Murder because it may be to your advantage to ask that it be considered by the judge or the jury during your trial.

---

[25] *Selby v. State*, 361 Md. 319, 332 (2000).
[26] Maryland Criminal Law § 2-207.
[27] *Dishman v. State*, 352 Md. 279, 287-288 (1998).

4.0. Maryland's Legal Uses of Force

In this section, we are going to discuss the four forms of legal uses of force that are recognized in the State of Maryland. These include Self-Defense, Defense of Others, Defense of Habitation and Defense of Property. As you can see the forms are not just personal self-defense, but include your right to protect others, your home, and your property.

There is a distinction between deadly and non-deadly force. Under Maryland law, deadly force is the amount of force that's reasonably calculated to cause death or serious bodily harm.[28] Non-deadly force is generally referred to as force. It is also important to know that in Maryland, simply brandishing deadly weapons can constitute the use of deadly force.

During the course of this chapter, we are going to give some examples of when deadly force or force generally can be used but for the reason previously stated, when we talked about how a case can turn on very slight details, it is important to take the examples with a grain of salt and talk to a lawyer you trust to get detailed answers to your detailed questions. The goal here is to educate you, the reader, about the law and give you a firm basis on which you can ask your favorite attorney your hypothetical. The overall rule, regardless of the degree of force, deadly or non-deadly, is that the use of force must be reasonable under the circumstances.

In Maryland, there are two levels of Defense of Self, Others and Habitation; (1) Perfect and (2) Imperfect, both of which will be explained in this chapter. The defendant always bears the initial burden of showing "some" evidence that all the elements of a form of legal use of force exist and then the burden shifts to the state's attorney to show that one or more of the elements are absent, or in the case of Imperfect Defense of Self, Others or

---

[28] See Maryland Pattern Jury Instruction 5:07 Self-Defense – "Deadly force is that amount of force reasonably calculated to cause death or serious bodily harm."

Habitation, which will be explained shortly, that the defendant's beliefs were unreasonable.[29] So, let's discuss what a defendant needs to show to be entitled to the protections of Maryland's forms of legal uses of force.

4.1. Perfect Self-Defense

Perfect Self-Defense is a complete defense to crimes like Murder and Assault.[30] If Self-Defense is found to apply, and the state's attorney has not met their burden of showing it doesn't, the defendant must be found not guilty. To successfully assert Perfect Self-Defense, the defense must first show "some" evidence:

1. That the defendant was not the aggressor, or in the case of deadly force, the defendant may be the aggressor, but they were not the one who raised the fight to the deadly force level;

2. The defendant actually believed that they were in immediate and imminent danger of bodily harm;

3. The defendant's belief was reasonable; and

4. The defendant used no more force than necessary to defend

---

[29] *Dykes v. State*, 319 Md. 206, 216-217 (1990) "Some evidence is not strictured by the test of a specific standard. It calls for no more than what it says 'some,' as that word is understood in common, everyday usage. It need not rise to the level of 'beyond reasonable doubt' or 'clear and convincing' or 'preponderance.' The source of the evidence is immaterial; it may emanate solely from the Defendant. It is of no matter that the self-defense claim is overwhelmed by evidence to the contrary. If there is any evidence relied on by the Defendant which, if believed, would support his claim that he acted in self-defense, the Defendant has met his burden. Then the baton is passed to the State. It must shoulder the burden of proving beyond a reasonable doubt to the satisfaction of the Jury that the Defendant did not kill in self-defense."

[30] See Maryland Pattern Jury Instruction 5:07 Self-Defense and 4:17.2 for self-defense/defense of others or habitation in Murder cases.

themselves in light of the threatened or actual harm.

And if the defendant is claiming Self-Defense in a situation where deadly force was used there is another element that needs to be addressed by the defendant:

5. The defendant is required to make an effort to retreat unless they fit within one of four exceptions.

4.1 a. Exceptions to the duty to retreat when using deadly force

The four exceptions to the duty to retreat are:

1. If you are in your own home;

2. The avenue of retreat was unsafe or unknown;

3. You are being robbed; or

4. You are lawfully arresting the victim.

4.1 a(i). In your own home

In Maryland being in your own home includes being inside your dwelling or in the area around your home referred to as curtilage.[31] Curtilage in Maryland means an area near the residence that harbors the intimate activities associated with the sanctity of the home and the privacies recognized by the community at large.[32] When determining whether an area outside the home qualifies as being curtilage the court will look to factors such as the distance between the home and the space being considered, whether the area is within an enclosure surrounding the home, i.e. fencing, the way the space is used, and the steps taken by the residents to protect the area from

---

[31] *Gainer v. State*, 40 Md. App. 382, 388
[32] *Brown v. State*, 75 Md. App. 22, 30 (1988).

being observed by passing people.[33] "Curtilage is determined by factors that bear upon whether an individual may expect that the area in question should be treated as the home itself."[34] If you are outside of your home and relying on curtilage to relieve you of the duty to retreat beware, areas commonly accessed by the public, although seemingly within the curtilage may be determined by the court to be non-curtilage, making you subject to the duty to retreat.[35]

4.1 a(ii). <u>Retreat was unsafe, or the route was unknown</u>

The second exception, retreat was unsafe, or the avenue of escape was unknown, is likely the most common exception. When someone is facing a situation where the use of force is necessary, they often cannot see a way out of the event. There are times when simply running or walking away is impossible due to the health of the user of force or the layout of the surrounding environment. Although this exception is the most common, it's also often forgotten when users of force report the situation. It is natural to want to talk about what the other person did that created the need to use force, but in the process, people forget to inform the police about things like how they know the doors were locked and they simply didn't know a way out. There is no doubt that your mind took those factors into account when you acted so be sure to provide that information as well should you choose to speak with the police.

4.1 a(iii). <u>The victim of a Robbery</u>

The third exception is that the user of force is the victim of a Robbery, and the Robbery is in progress.[36] It is critical to understand what a Robbery is in Maryland. It is the taking of

---

[33] *Id.*
[34] *United States v. Dunn*, 480 U.S. 294, 300 (1987).
[35] *Brown* at 33.
[36] *Sydnor v. State*, 133 Md. App. 173, 187-188 (2000).

property from a person by force or fear.[37] Unfortunately, people who are not trained in the law say things like "my house got robbed" when they are describing what the law of Maryland would call a Burglary or Theft. A Burglary occurs when someone breaks and enters your home and unlike a Robbery it does not require you to be present when the breaking and entering occurs. To be protected by this exception the Robbery must meet Maryland's legal definition of a Robbery, and not merely be a Theft of some sort that has been mislabeled as a Robbery by someone who doesn't understand what the law requires. Maryland law does not allow a person to use deadly force to protect property so knowing the distinction between Robbery and Theft can be the difference between a not guilty verdict and serious jail time for someone who uses deadly force in a use of force situation.

The Robbery exception to the duty to retreat can create perilous legal issues. Such as, once a Robbery is completed, for example the property is taken, the exception falls away, and if another exception to the duty to retreat does not apply, the duty to retreat is reinstated. This highlights the importance of speaking with an attorney prior to speaking with the police or else a person may risk neglecting to report the facts that mandated the continued use of deadly force after the completion of the Robbery and ultimately walk themselves into an unwarranted conviction for a serious crime.

---

[37] See Maryland Criminal Law § 3-402 Robbery and § 3-403 Robbery with a dangerous weapon see also *Fetrow v. State*, 156 Md. App. 675, 687 "Under Maryland law, '[r]obbery is the felonious taking and carrying away of the personal property of another from his person by the use of violence or by putting in fear'." Note that the robbery exception does not require that the robber be armed in order to relieve the user of force of the duty to retreat but the judge or jury will still be required to determine whether the degree of force used was reasonable.

4.1 a(iv). <u>Lawfully arresting the victim</u>[38]

Private citizens in Maryland can arrest a person without a warrant when[39]:

1. In the case of felonies - there has been either a felony committed in their presence or there has in fact been a felony committed, whether it occurred in their presence, and the arrester has probable cause to believe the person they are arresting committed it; or

2. In the case of misdemeanors – that there is a misdemeanor being committed in the presence of the arrester and the misdemeanor amounts to a disturbance of the public peace. Breach of the public peace means "disorderly, dangerous conduct, 'an affray, actual violence, or conduct tending to or provocative of violence by others'".[40]

One needs to be careful about making citizen arrests, especially when they themselves are not directly involved in the initial situation because things can appear to be vastly different from what they truly are. Judges and juries highly disfavor vigilante-style behavior especially when there was ample time and opportunity to contact the police. Stopping a store robbery and detaining a robber may be praised while confronting a group of kids who, in the opinion of the arrester, appear to be disturbing the public peace may be perceived as being aggressive and unnecessary.

---

[38] Police officers and private citizens differ slightly in this regard. This writing will focus on the rights of a private citizen because a police officer SHOULD know the parameters of their powers when operating within their jurisdiction. When operating outside of their jurisdiction the parameters discussed within apply to police officers.
[39] *Stevenson v. State*, 287 Md. 504, 512 (1980).
[40] *Spry v. State*, 396 Md. 682, 691 (2007).

4.1 a(v). Concluding thoughts on the Duty to Retreat

Once again, the failure to make a reasonable effort to retreat when such an effort is required by law is an absolute bar to the assertion of Self-Defense although one may still assert other forms of legal uses of force as explained later. It is imperative that information pertaining to retreat or reasons for not retreating be provided, when necessary, whether in an initial report to the police or at trial.

4.1 b. Who must prove what in a Self-Defense case

Under Maryland law, a defendant asserting Self-Defense must first show there is "some" evidence that all the previously stated factors exist and then the burden is on the state's attorney to prove at least one of the factors is absent.[41] Note that the defendant's burden of proving these factors is not great, meaning you do not have to prove beyond a reasonable doubt that they exist, the defendant simply needs to put on "some" evidence of each of the factors and the burden shifts to the state to prove one of the factors doesn't exist at all. This requirement that the defendant put on "some" evidence of each of the elements is applicable to every form of legal use of force found in Maryland.

Under Maryland law, if the judge or jury determines the defendant was the aggressor, was the first to raise the force to the deadly force level or that the defendant didn't believe they were in danger of serious bodily harm or worse, the defendant loses a self-defense argument. Also, if both parties, the user of force and the "victim" are willing combatants the court may rule that both are aggressors, and neither is entitled to assert a form of legally justified use of force.[42]

---

[41] *Dykes* at 216 (1990).
[42] *Whitehead v. State*, 9 Md. App. 7, 13 (1970) the court found that provocation reduced the Murder charge to Manslaughter but did not allow the application of self-defense due to the fact that the defendant told the decedent "if we are going to fight, let's go

Use of Force cases can turn who is labeled the aggressor but what this means is almost made on a case-by-case basis. Determining who is the aggressor is generally left to the judge or jury to decide, based on their own opinions, because the law in Maryland offers little guidance as to how to determine if someone is an aggressor. This is another example of why speaking with an attorney before the police could be critical to making sure all the facts necessary to support your legal use of force claim are brought out.

The best advice in this situation is the bigger the stick you carry, the softer you should speak. The feebler the person, the less likely they are to be labeled the aggressor despite being loud, aggressive, or even violent.[43]

4.2. Imperfect Self-Defense

Imperfect Self-Defense is when the defendant has put up evidence of each of the elements of Perfect Self-Defense, but the state's attorney is able to prove to a judge or jury that the degree of force used was unreasonable or that the defendant's belief of imminent bodily harm or their belief that retreat was unsafe was unreasonable. If the state's attorney convinces a judge or jury that Imperfect Self-Defense applies, a judge or jury is instructed in a Murder case to find that the proper verdict is guilty of Voluntary Manslaughter, which carries a maximum penalty of 10 years or in a case involving Assault in the First Degree the proper verdict is Assault in the Second Degree which also carries 10 years.[44] Please note that if a firearm was used in the commission of Voluntary Manslaughter or Assault in the Second Degree an

---

outside" at which point both parties went outside and engaged in a fight that resulted in the death of the decedent.

[43] *Maddran v. Mullendore*, 206 Md. 291, 300 (1955).

[44] See *Dykes* at 212 in reference to Murder's conversion to Voluntary Manslaughter and *Christian v. State*, 405 Md. 306, 333 (2008) pertaining to Assault in the First Degree's conversion to Assault in the Second Degree.

additional 20 years could be imposed for Use of a Firearm in the Commission of a Felony or Crime of Violence, as explained earlier. Imperfect use of force is not limited to specifically Self-Defense and can also apply to cases involving the Defense of Others or Habitation.

4.3. Defense of Others

In Maryland, you are allowed to use force in the defense of others.[45] Defense of Others can be a Perfect or Imperfect defense as is found in Self-Defense.

The process of determining whether a person is entitled to this defense mirrors that of Self-Defense, whereby the user is mandated to show "some" evidence of each of the elements first and then the burden shifts to the state's attorney to prove the absence or unreasonableness of elements.

The use of force in the defense of others requires:

1. That the defendant actually believed that the person he was defending was in immediate and imminent danger of death or serious bodily harm;

2. The defendant's belief was reasonable;

3. The defendant used no more force than was reasonably necessary in light of the threatened or actual force; and

4. The defendant's purpose in using force was to aid the person they were defending.

---

[45] See Maryland Pattern Jury Instruction 4:17.3 for Defense of Others in the context of Murder and Maryland Pattern Jury Instruction 5:01 for Defense of Others in all other cases.

As previously explained in the context of Self-Defense, if the state's attorney can show that the defendant's belief, or the degree of force used, was unreasonable, the verdict results in what is known as Imperfect Defense of Others and will mitigate Murder to Voluntary Manslaughter and Assault in the First Degree to Assault in the Second Degree, but will not completely vindicate the user. Defense of Others does not require proof of who was the aggressor, nor does it impose a duty to retreat as a matter of law, as does Self-Defense. Maryland law seems to recognize that a citizen may stumble upon an event in progress and need to act without an opportunity to assess who started the conflict. Despite that, it remains a common practice for the state's attorney to argue that their "victim" was the non-aggressor or that the defendant was jumping into a mutually consented to and otherwise fair fight.

4.4. Defense of Habitation

In Maryland you have a right to use deadly force to defend your home under certain circumstances.[46] This right is sometimes referred to as the "castle doctrine".[47] In order to be protected under Maryland law the defendant needs to show "some" evidence:

1. That the perpetrator entered or attempted to enter their home;

2. That the defendant believed the perpetrator intended to commit a crime that would involve an imminent threat of death or serious bodily harm;

---

[46] See Maryland Pattern Jury Instruction 4:17.3 for Defense of Habitation in the context of Murder and Maryland Pattern Jury Instruction 5:02 Defense of Habitation – Deadly force. Go to Defense of Property discussed in section 4.5 if non-deadly force is used.
[47] *Gainer v. State*, 40 Md. App. 382 (1978).

3. That the defendant reasonably believed that the perpetrator intended to commit such a crime;

4. That the defendant believed the use of force used was necessary to prevent imminent death or serious bodily harm; and

5. The defendant reasonably believed that such force was necessary.

As with the previous forms of legally justified uses of force, the defendant bears the initial burden of showing "some" evidence supporting each one of the previously stated factors and then the burden shifts to the state's attorney to prove beyond a reasonable doubt that one of the factors is absent. Like Self-Defense, if a judge or jury was to find that the defendant's belief that the perpetrator posed an imminent threat of death or serious bodily harm was sincere, but unreasonable, the law of Maryland says the verdict should be guilty of Voluntary Manslaughter in a case where Murder is charged and Assault in the Second Degree where the allegation is Assault in the First Degree.

The first element of the Defense of Habitation requires that the perpetrator entered, or attempted to enter, the defendant's home. The term "entered" is fairly self-explanatory but attempt under Maryland law has a very specific definition that is important to explain. Maryland law defines attempt as "an intent to commit a particular offense coupled with some overt act in furtherance of the intent which goes beyond mere preparation".[48] Although many situations arise where we may know the intent of a nefarious actor, the law will not allow us to resort to force of any type in defense of habitation without the nefarious actor doing an act that puts their intent on full display.

---

[48] *Cox v. State*, 311 Md. 326, 330 (1988).

In some cases in order to prove an attempted entry in accordance with the first element of Defense of Habitation some fact-finders, judges or jurors, may want to see that the perpetrator was actually caught climbing in a window or breaking a door and it is probable that a state's attorney will argue that the perpetrator's mere presence on your property is not enough to allow the judge or jury to consider Defense of Habitation as a defense at all, although other forms of legal use of force may apply. So be aware that although attempt has a legal definition it remains a vague term subject to different interpretations by different judges or juries when applied to the facts of specific cases.

4.4a. Trespassers

What about getting a trespasser to leave? In Maryland, you are allowed to use reasonable force to expel a trespasser.[49] A trespasser is a person who enters or crosses over the private property of another, without a legal reason to do so, after having been notified by the owner not to do so. In non-deadly force situations, you can put a trespasser out using any means that doesn't constitute a breach of the public peace, as that term was previously explained in section 4.1a4.[50] That is a lot of legal jargon so let's break it down.

You can remove a trespasser from your property if it is NOT:

1. Unreasonable force: i.e., throwing a frail old lady off an elevated porch or pointing a gun at an unarmed person; or

---

[49] *Maddran* at 299-300 (1955).
[50] Breach of the public peace means "disorderly, dangerous conduct, 'an affray, actual violence, or conduct tending to or provocative of violence by others'." *Spry* at 691.

2. Disorderly or Dangerous: i.e., yelling in the middle of the night in a neighborhood full of sleeping families or fighting in public with the trespasser.

4.5. Defense of Property

The number one rule about exercising your right to defend property is that you cannot use deadly force of any kind.[51] It doesn't matter that the person is breaking into your classic car and stealing your mother's wedding ring that was passed down through three generations of your family, you cannot use anything that could cause death or serious bodily harm to defend those things. But Maryland law does allow you to use force in the defense of your possessions.

To be protected under Maryland law the defense would need to show:

1. That defendant actually believed that the perpetrator was unlawfully or was just about to unlawfully interfere with the defendant's property;

2. That the defendant's belief was reasonable; and

3. That the defendant used no more force than was reasonably necessary to defend against the perpetrator's interference with their property.

In Defense of Property situations, the goal is to stop the interference with your property and once that purpose is served this defense no longer applies so one must be careful to cease acting the moment the interference has been abated. In the case of a Robbery, where someone has used force or fear to take

---

[51] See Maryland Pattern Jury Instruction 5:02.1 for elements which contains bracketed language stating that deadly force may not be used to defend property as well as the notes on use directing the Court to use the bracketed language if there is a factual issue as to whether deadly force used was in defense of property.

property from someone else, once the taking is accomplished by the robber, the victim's efforts to recover the property could be deemed Defense of Property and subject to the prohibition on the use of deadly force.[52] Although the robbery was over, the situation could have converted to one where the defendant was attempting to lawfully arrest the perpetrator thus once again creating the potential for the legal use of deadly force and alleviating the duty to retreat. This type of rapidly unfolding and convoluted scenario highlights the importance of speaking with an attorney prior to making any statements to the police concerning any use of force, especially deadly force, because the forms of legal use of force can overlap and carry different requirements.

---

[52] See generally *Sydnor v. State*, 133 Md. App. 173 (2000).

5.0. You had to use force – Now what happens

The purpose of this chapter is to help you understand the common court procedures following a use of force situation and give you an idea of what to expect procedurally. People need to understand that every case is different and there is no checklist that one can use to guarantee they will not be charged or even convicted of a crime and every case and courthouse moves at its own speed meaning many cases can take months or even years to work their way through the criminal justice system. A person who uses force needs to prepare themselves to deal with a stressful situation for what can be an extended period of time.

5.1. Assume that everything is recorded

It seems odd to start a discussion about what follows a use of force event with a focus on recordings and not an interaction with the police or something similar, but in the chronology of events in a use of force case it is common for there to be videos of what occurred during, or immediately afterwards, and before the police are contacted or arrive on the scene. In our world today, for better or worse, everything is recorded. In many cases it is to your benefit the fact that there is a wide range of recorded data available, but sometimes it's complicated getting the data we need.

5.1 a. Surveillance Footage

Something like surveillance footage, for example, is often only stored for limited amounts of time and sometimes determining who owns the cameras, has access to the cameras and can provide the footage is a daunting task. For example, there can be situations where the owner and the operator of the camera are two separate and distinct people or companies. Also, since anything you say or do before, during or after a use of force event may have been recorded it is imperative that you act appropriately and take time to note things like the camera locations or other devices that may have captured information relevant to your case and provide that information immediately to your attorney.

5.1 b. <u>911 Calls and Body Camera Footage</u>

In Maryland, 911 calls and most in-person interactions with responding police officers are recorded. What you say on a 911 call or to the officers that respond to a call will be forever memorialized and available for court. Police officers are generally supposed to tell everyone they are being recorded on their body cameras but sometimes they don't. In all fairness to police officers, there are times when they arrive and someone is badly injured, those are times where notifying people about a running body camera takes a back seat to securing the scene and arranging the transport of the injured person to a hospital. The real lesson here is that the police are likely recording everything someone on the scene says even when the police haven't formally announced that the cameras are on.

In reference to 911 calls specifically, there is no law requiring a person to contact 911 in the event of a use of force. You may have noticed as we went through the elements of the various forms of legal use of force at no point did the law require the user to have sought police or medical assistance for themselves or the other party. It is rare that a person who contacted 911 immediately is convicted of crimes like Murder but that does not make calling 911 a legal requirement to be entitled to the protections of Maryland's use of force laws and in many cases, people don't contact 911 for reasons that are consistent with innocence. Although that is the law, judges and juries tend to give the benefit of the doubt to those who call 911 and/or speak with the police and struggle with the idea that someone did not.

If you contact 911, keep in mind that everything is being recorded, including which number contacted 911, and it is ok to simply tell the operator that there is an injured person or that police are needed, give the location and hang up since 911 will dispatch responders to the location based on that nominal information.

Many police departments also have cameras installed in and around their vehicles that allow them to record anything that is happening around the squad car. Parties involved in use of force situations are regularly told to stand near or placed in squad cars while the on-scene investigation takes place, and what may seem like a quiet place to sit alone with your thoughts is really a recording studio waiting for you to say or do anything that can be used to prosecute you.

5.1c. Jail Calls

Jail calls are also recorded. When a person is arrested it is common for their first call to be to family members who inevitably ask "what happened" or if they have some knowledge of the mechanics of the event, family members will make comments regarding the matter. It is not just jail call confessions that make their way into the courtroom. There are times when a judge will allow the state's attorney to play jail calls containing statements someone made to you, but you did not refute or deny under the guise that you adopted the statement. So, it is very important that your case is not discussed at all on the jail phone by any party, yourself or the person you are speaking to, or you run the risk of the state's attorney taking comments out of context and using them against you.

In addition, family members and friends often try to use the three-way calling feature to contact lawyers, with both you and them thinking they are doing you a service. The problem is that the call is being monitored in that situation, attorney-client privilege may not apply due to the presence of other people on the call, and many times your lawyer doesn't even realize why they are getting the call in the first place, putting them in a very awkward position. In some Maryland jurisdictions, attorneys can set up calls with clients quickly, and those calls are not monitored, or in all jurisdictions an attorney can go and visit a client, so the immediate cold call, where your case is discussed, is unnecessary and risky.

5.2. Speaking with the Police

There is no right answer as to whether you should speak with the police. A lawyer can only say that you're not required under Maryland law to speak with the police. Nor are you required to stay on the scene in a use of force situation as one can see from the elements of the various forms of legal use of force discussed earlier.[53] People who remain on the scene and speak with the police immediately are generally favored by judges and juries but if you talk to the police and do not provide the requisite information to support your use of force, or worse, give information that negates the legal use of force claim, being favored can only go so far. As with 911 calls, juries, and sometimes even judges, seem to struggle with situations where the defendant did not speak with the police after a use of force event, despite the defendant's constitutional right to remain silent.

State's attorneys are not allowed to use your silence against you in most circumstances, but they are always allowed to use your freely and voluntarily made statements if they think it will further a case against you and get you convicted. Under Maryland law state's attorneys are not required to play your previous statement in court if it is helpful to you so understand that even if you do speak with police and explain everything to prove a legally justified use of force under Maryland law you may still have an uphill battle if you want to play your earlier

---

[53] See Maryland Pattern Jury Instruction 3:24 Flight or Concealment of Defendant - which says that flight may be motivated by a variety of factors, some of which are fully consistent with innocence and then asks the jury to consider whether there is evidence of flight and if so whether the flight shows consciousness of guilt.

recorded statement to either the judge or jury at trial.

If it is your choice to speak with the police, you should undoubtedly speak with a lawyer prior to any discussions and reasonable police officers will facilitate this. If you are in police custody, a clear and unequivocal invocation of your right to counsel requires that the police must cease further questioning until counsel is obtained and is present. A voluntary re-initiation of a conversation with the police waives your assertion of your right to remain silent.[54] You should assert your right to counsel and speak with a lawyer prior to any questioning even if it will result in your transport to a station or jail. If a police officer will not allow you to speak with your attorney before speaking with them, they are unreasonable and probably wouldn't have listened to what you had to say anyways.

5.2a. What can happen during your interactions with the police

In the beginning phases of an investigation police officers will approach and ask what happened. During this phase, there are times when the police do not need to advise anyone of their right to remain silent because they do not have anyone in custody.[55] The so-called *Miranda* rights, the litany read off by police officers to arrestees concerning their right to remain silent, isn't required if the person is not in custody and being questioned by police.[56]

Knowing this, depending on the dynamics of any given situation, police officers have ways of trying to elicit as much information as possible prior to arresting a person or placing them in custody. A police officer is trained to work within and

---

[54] *Davis v. United States*, 512 U.S. 452, 458 (1994).
[55] *Cummings v. State*, 27 Md. App. 361, 370-371 (1975).
[56] *Miranda v. Arizona*, 384 U.S. 436 (1966).

around your 5th Amendment right to remain silent and will use this training to try to make a case if they feel like there is a case to be made. This is not a jab at police officers - lawyers too are taught the very same thing. Without the same training a person may find themselves at a disadvantage in a discussion with the police. This can be exceptionally treacherous when combined with the fact that police officers are legally allowed to skew the truth and even lie during these conversations or interrogations.

The most important thing to remember is that when you're speaking with the police you can say I want to stop, and they "should" stop the conversation right there on the spot. The word "should" is used in that sentence because there are times when a police officer will use some form of coercion to continue the conversation, despite your request to stop, and if the court rules you are "not in custody" and/or you voluntarily reinitiated the conversation the state may be allowed to use your later statements against you. The term coercion is not meant to mean that the police are doing something nefarious but to refer to situations where your free will could be affected by the actions or statements of the police.

Common forms of coercion include asking the person if they have any questions in an effort to extend the conversation, not explaining what is occurring or what charges the person faces, arrest or cuffing, retention of property for investigative purposes, statements by the officer alluding to what other witnesses said or the evidence showed or, in the case where the person has requested an attorney, statements by the officer indicating that there will be plenty of time for that later but not right now.

Police officers can, and often do, allow people to speak with attorneys. Our office has been involved with several cases where a police officer has given the person a private space to speak with us on the phone, on the scene of the event, and in none of those cases were any of those statements offered as evidence during the pendency of a case, if one was even brought. We have also been able to meet with and privately discuss the case with clients who have been transported to police stations for questioning and once again, as of this writing, there has not been an instance where the state's attorney attempted to use any part of those discussions in court.

5.3. The media may be interested in your case

People seem surprised when it happens, but the media may take interest in your case. There are times when the media will just show up at your house or at a family member's house, wherever they you think you may be, and start talking with anyone who will talk to them. People should avoid talking to the media for the same reason explained earlier, the media wants sensationalism. You should speak with your attorney about whether a press conference or public address of some sort is warranted in your case.

5.4. Do you charge the other party or not

In the cases involving Self-Defense, Defense of Habitation or Property – you are the victim. In some situations, you may need to decide whether to file charges against the other party, or seek other relief, for the crimes they committed against you. But as with most decisions there are reasons for and against doing so. The decision of whether to begin court proceedings against the other party can be critical and should be made with the assistance of an attorney who understands the facts of your case. A lawyer can explain the filing process and other considerations. Time is of the essence when deciding whether to file charges against the other party because often the longer it takes for someone to file charges the more likely it is that the state's attorney will elect not to prosecute the other side.

5.4 a. Peace and Protective Orders

In a use of force case, you could be on either side of a peace or protective order. The law regarding peace and protective orders can be rather tedious so this writing will merely be an overview. As with any aspect of legally justified uses of force, discussion with an attorney about the specifics of any given case is essential.

In both a peace or protective order, the court can order a person to do various things, including but not limited to, staying away from specific people and locations and even order that people turn their firearms over to law enforcement.[57]

A protective order can be sought in a case where the party filing for the order is a "person eligible for relief". A "person eligible for relief" is usually someone in a familial, sexual or co-habitation type of relationship with the other party, although there are other qualifications available, and the person filing alleges a form of "abuse", as defined under Maryland law, occurred.[58]

If someone does not qualify as a "person eligible for relief" and thus a protective order, they can file for what is known as a peace order. Peace orders can be filed when someone alleges one or more specific acts listed in Maryland law have occurred against them in the last 30 days.[59]

If you are considering filing a peace or protective order, or defending yourself against one, working with an attorney is imperative because although the hearing seems to be conducted in an informal manner, you may be giving statements or

---

[57] Md. Family Law § 4-506 Final Protective Orders generally.
[58] See Maryland Family Law § 4-501 Definitions (b)(1) defining "Abuse" and (m) defining "Person Eligible for Relief".
[59] See Maryland Courts and Judicial Proceedings § 3-1503.1 - Interim Peace Orders and § 3-1505 - Final Peace Orders.

evidence that can be used against you in any criminal case and if not given properly that evidence could be misconstrued at that hearing or in future proceedings. There may be times your attorney will advise you to remain silent, to not produce evidence or to even consent to the filing of an order against you in an effort to win the case where you are charged with a crime.

A lawyer is never allowed to tell a client what to say, but a lawyer can help them understand what the law requires and prepare them to testify. If your case is asserting a legal use of force defense and you are charging the other party or involved with a peace or protective order, it is imperative that you work with an attorney so you can make sure to produce the proper information to substantiate your claim.

5.5. What will happen as my case moves through the system

This section will explain the general flow of how things will work regarding use of force cases in Maryland. Keep in mind that there is always some glitch, and every jurisdiction and case is different. Most of the charges referenced previously were felonies so this section will focus primarily on how felony cases move through the system with the major distinction being that misdemeanor cases, such as Assault in the Second Degree and Reckless Endangerment, can be tried in the District Court or, if the defendant faces a maximum penalty in excess of 90 days, the defendant can ask that their case be forwarded to the Circuit Court for trial in what is commonly referred to as a jury trial prayer.[60] A case tried in the District Court that results in a guilty finding can be appealed by the defendant, and that appeal is heard, as a brand new trial or what is known as *de novo*, in the Circuit Court of the jurisdiction where the case was tried.[61] If you are charged with misdemeanor offenses you should discuss

---

[60] Maryland Courts and Judicial Proceedings § 4-302 Exceptions to jurisdiction.
[61] Maryland Courts and Judicial Proceedings § 12-401 Appeals permitted.

the jury trial prayer option with your attorney, including the benefits and risks.

5.5a. Charging

Whether you are charged with felonies or misdemeanors the formal legal process starts with some form of arrest, a warrant or a summons that is issued, which gets you charged. You might be arrested; the court could mail you a letter telling you to come to court or the court may send you a letter telling you to report to the court commissioner's office. If you find that a warrant has been put out for your arrest an attorney can assist you with making efforts to have that warrant recalled, or what is known as quashed, so that you don't have to be arrested.

After the initial charging process, in most cases you will have a commissioner hearing. A commissioner hearing is when you appear before the court commissioner as we discussed in section 2.3. The court commissioner determines if there is probable cause to charge you with whatever crimes are alleged, they then tell you what the maximum penalties are for the charges, that you have a right to get an attorney, the process by which you can get an attorney appointed if you can't afford one and, when charged with felonies, they will ask you if you want a preliminary hearing. The answer to the last question is always yes because you can waive the request for a preliminary hearing later.[62] The court commissioner also decides what your bail status should be which can include being released on your own recognizance, held on a monetary bail or held without bail. In the State of Maryland, defendants are entitled to have an attorney represent them at their commissioner hearing, and attorneys often do, unless the defendant waives their right to counsel. A waiver for the commissioner hearing is not a waiver

---

[62] See Maryland Rule 4-213 Initial Appearance of the Defendant.

of counsel for the rest of the case, it is just a waiver for that specific hearing.

If the commissioner holds you without bail or holds you with bail that you can't pay, then you are supposed to have a bail review in front of a judge in the District Court of Maryland the next day the court is available.[63] There are times when an arrest occurs late at night or on the weekend, and you may not appear on the District Court bail review docket for a couple days.

Bail reviews are interesting because there really is no set process that is followed. The law requires the judge to set the least onerous conditions for release and the considerations the judge must use but exactly how that determination is made varies from judge to judge.[64] Some judges will allow witnesses to speak on the defendant's behalf, some will allow minitrials about the facts of the case or history of involved parties and others won't allow any of that. In preparation for your bail review it is important to provide your attorney with proof of a stable address, at a location that will allow you to remain away from the "victim" or "state's witnesses", and proof of employment, if possible. If a defendant is held after their bail review, there are a couple of ways to seek a re-review of bail, but these methods vary from jurisdiction to jurisdiction.

5.5b. District and Circuit Courts

In Maryland there are two parts to the court system, the District Court of Maryland and the Circuit Court of whatever county the incident is alleged to have taken place in. The relationship between the District and Circuit Courts can be complicated so this section will simply offer an overview and a

---

[63] There are times when a case will have its first bail review in the Circuit Court but that is far less common.
[64] Maryland Rule 4-216.1 Pretrial Release – Standards Governing.

discussion with your attorney can clarify how this relationship works in a specific case.

One could view the District Court as the lower of the two court systems, District Court and Circuit Court, but this is not a completely accurate portrayal of the system. The District Court seems lower to many defendants because cases tend to start there and end at the Circuit Court, but the reality is that both the District and Circuit Court have responsibilities that make both critical to the operation of the criminal justice system.

5.5b(i). District Court

The District Court of Maryland on the State level is different from the federal United States District Courts located in Baltimore City and Greenbelt. Each Maryland county and Baltimore City has one or more state District Courts, and they are often smaller courthouses where judges decide the cases. In the District Court, jury trials are not conducted. Most felony cases cannot be brought to trial in the District Court although things like bail reviews and preliminary hearings connected to such cases can be conducted there.

5.5b(ii). Circuit Court

There is a Circuit Court building or complex in each Maryland county and Baltimore City. The Circuit Court buildings tend to be larger than their District Court counterparts due to the need to accommodate jurors. Most felonies are required to be tried at the Circuit Court and there the defendants can elect to have their trial decided by either a judge or jury.

5.5c. Preliminary Hearings and Grand Juries

If you are charged with felonies, the next step in the process is either a preliminary hearing, which is a public hearing almost universally conducted in the District Court of Maryland, during which the judge decides if there is probable cause to forward your case to Circuit Court where most felonies are required by law to conduct their trials, or, if a grand jury hears your case, that proceeding is conducted behind closed doors, without your presence, and the grand jury decides whether your pending felony charges should be forwarded to Circuit Court for trial.[65]

There are times when a case is scheduled for a preliminary hearing, but the defendant waives their right to such a hearing and the matter is forwarded to the Circuit Court by the consent of the defendant. You should discuss this option with your attorney if a preliminary hearing is scheduled to help you decide if this would be helpful to your case.

People tend to get frustrated if their matter is indicted by a grand jury or forwarded to the Circuit Court after a preliminary hearing thinking that this means they will be found guilty. The truth is the burden of proof and rules of evidence at a preliminary hearing or at the grand jury are so different from those at a trial that an indictment forwarding your case to Circuit Court means in no way that you will be convicted.[66] Also, since jury trials are exclusively held in the Circuit Court, it may be preferable to have your case in the Circuit Court where you can choose to have either a judge or a jury decide your case.

5.5d. Arraignments and Initial Appearances

Arraignments and initial appearances are scheduling conferences where you plead not guilty, you are advised of the maximum penalties you face in the Circuit Court, your right to a jury trial and court dates are set on the calendar. Most Maryland jurisdictions no longer have in-person arraignments and instead the case is removed from the arraignment docket when a defense attorney enters their appearance telling the

---

[65] Maryland Rule 4-221 Preliminary Hearing in District Court.
[66] Maryland Rule 5-101(b)(1) and (7) Scope – make the rules of evidence generally inapplicable to grand jury proceedings and preliminary hearings.

court that they will be representing the defendant. If the case is removed due to an entry of appearance by defense counsel, the defendant's attorney will then get in contact with the state's attorney to pick dates for court appearances and submit the dates to the court for scheduling. In some jurisdictions, Murder cases are assigned to a specific judge almost right from the beginning and all scheduling needs to be approved by them.

5.5e. Pretrial Motions

Leading up to trial, depending on what jurisdiction you are in, and which judge your case is assigned to, the court may schedule a pretrial motions hearing. A pretrial motions hearing usually involves whether certain evidence should be deemed admissible or inadmissible at trial. Some motions, such as motions to suppress evidence pursuant to the 4th Amendment or statements made by the defendant pursuant to the 5th Amendment must be filed in writing in advance of trial while other motions, known as motions *in limine* are where a party can ask the court to admit or deny the admission of certain evidence, at almost any phase of the trial, based on other rules of evidence.

Having motions to suppress evidence or motions *in limine* decided prior to trial is important because it gives the attorneys time to adjust the presentation of evidence to the rulings of the court and prevents surprises during trial. Also, handling motions in advance of trial allows the parties to obtain transcripts of witnesses' testimony that could be helpful during the trial itself.

5.5f. Trial

As you move towards your trial date one of the decisions you will need to make is whether you wish to have a bench or jury trial. In a bench trial, the judge decides guilt. In a jury trial, twelve people selected from the licensed drivers, holders of Maryland state issued identifications and registered Maryland voters that reside in the county where the case will be tried, decide the case. In a jury trial, all twelve members of the jury must agree on the verdict, meaning all twelve must say either guilty or not guilty, and if they cannot agree on a verdict it results in a hung jury which allows the state's attorney to retry the case over and over until either the jury comes back with a unanimous verdict, or the state's attorney grows tired of trying the case. It is not unheard of that a case can be tried three or more times before there is a unanimous verdict in a jury trial. In the State of Maryland, the defendant alone gets to make the decision of whether to have a bench or a jury trial and doesn't need the approval of anyone else. It is important to discuss the risks and benefits of both types of trials with your attorney.

If you elect to have a jury trial, jury selection will begin. Jury selection can be a lengthy process and becomes even longer the more serious the case is. Generally, the process is one where questions are asked of a large group of potential jurors, either in writing or out loud in the courtroom, followed by more specific questions asked of those who answered the earlier questions in a way that piqued the interest of the court. Jurors that are unable to be fair and impartial should be removed by way of what is known as a strike for cause. Once the pool of purportedly fair and impartial jurors has been established the next step is to have jurors brought up and the state's attorney and the defense can use what is known as peremptory strikes, which are discretionary strikes allotted to the parties to use at will. The number of peremptory strikes differs based on the maximum penalties the defendant faces and cannot be used by either party to remove a juror simply based on race or gender.[67]

During jury selection a defendant may be asked to stand and face the pool of potential jurors so they can determine whether

---

[67] *Batson v. Kentucky*, 106 S.Ct. 1712 (1986) prohibited the use of preemptory strikes based on race and this was later extended to gender in *J.E.B. v. Alabama ex rel. T.B.*, 511 U.S. 127 (1994).

they know or have knowledge of the person on trial. Regardless of whether that occurs during selection the jurors will spend a significant amount of time staring at the defendant. It is important to be aware that they are watching and listening to everything happening at the defense table and to dress and act accordingly.

5.5f(i). Opening statement by the state's attorney and witnesses

You can expect the state's attorney to talk about you like a wild animal. You may hear things like "the defendant shot nine times, one time wasn't good enough, he shot him in the head and heart and chased him for seventy-five feet and he didn't try to retreat, the defendant himself said he didn't, and the video shows he didn't. The defendant was the aggressor." Prosecutors tend to be more aggressive in cases where there are allegations involving violent crimes, but the jury has not heard the whole trial yet so do not let their words rattle you.

In almost every Murder trial, the medical examiner gets on the stand and testifies about the autopsy performed on the "victim" and displays pictures of the "victims" body and in a similar vein during most cases involving serious bodily injuries to the "victim", medical records and/or photographs of injuries are displayed in open court. Be prepared for such testimony or evidence because it is common for people in the courtroom to become emotional during such displays.

5.5.f(ii). Putting on your case

With all legally recognized uses of force in Maryland the burden is on the defendant to show "some" evidence to support each of the requirements that make up the defense and once that is accomplished the burden then shifts to the state's attorney to show beyond a reasonable doubt that those requirements were not met.

Although the law cannot require a defendant to testify, produce evidence, or put on a defense during a trial, in Maryland when a defendant asserts a form of legal use of force it can feel like that basic premise of our criminal justice system is out the window. Defense witnesses, physical evidence such as videos, text messages and other recordings and even the testimony of the defendant themself can become necessary components of the defense. There are times when the defendant can meet the initial burden discussed above by and through witnesses or physical evidence produced by the state's attorney and has no need to call witnesses or produce evidence themselves, but those times are few and far between. Often it is critical that the defendant provides the information necessary to move their defense forward. Earlier we discussed how in our modern world cameras abound, but the time in which their footage is retained can be very limited, and that can be coupled with the fact that witnesses that are excited to give statements when an event occurs fade away the longer a case is pending making it all the more important that you discuss any potential evidence that could be relevant to your defense immediately with your attorney. By promptly bringing this information to the attention of your attorney the proper filings and investigations can be made to ensure your ability to use beneficial evidence at trial.

5.5.f(iii). Testifying at trial

At trial you have the absolute right to remain silent and no duty to testify, but because the burden is on the defense to show "some" evidence of all the elements of a form of legal use of force before it can be considered by either the judge or the jury it may be impossible to meet the initial burden without testifying. As a case proceeds through the criminal justice system, there are often lulls in activity, times when it seems like your case is just on a shelf and nothing is happening, but for you that can be far from the truth. This is a great time for you to become acquainted with the evidence in your case and to go over any statements made to the police. Once the state's attorney delivers a copy of your discovery, discovery being the evidence the state's attorney is required to turn over by law, you should obtain a copy. If you are not incarcerated, you can take a computer thumb drive or external drive to your lawyer's office and obtain a copy of all the discovery and if you are incarcerated your attorney should have a copy delivered to you. Being incarcerated is a significant hinderance to preparing your case because you may not have easy access to recordings such as the body camera footage and recorded statements and as a result you may need transcripts or detailed notes to be produced that will allow you to read what witnesses and even you yourself reported during the investigation.

Once you receive the discovery, you should become familiar with all the statements you made that are in the possession of the state. This can be done on your own time. Having intimate knowledge of what you previously said will make preparing to testify substantially easier when you meet with your attorney.

Generally, it is a good practice to meet with your attorney:

1. Before discovery is provided to give them an idea of what to look for;

2. After discovery is provided to review the discovery together;

3. Later meet to go over testimony and witnesses generally and establish a general flow to how trial and testifying will work; and

4. Lastly, around the trial date to deal with specific points and how exhibits might fit into the defense's case and your testimony.

The number of meetings can fluctuate depending on the case, but these four phases can be critical in making your testimony highlight the defense you are asserting. As previously stated, a lawyer is never allowed to tell a client what to say, but that doesn't mean that a lawyer shouldn't help their client understand what the law requires and help them present a case that meets those requirements. The state's attorney will do the same with their witnesses as well.

Do not be surprised if your attorney asks pointed and tough questions of you during the preparation for your trial testimony. Your attorney should do this to get you ready for the questions the state's attorney will likely ask as well as the way they may ask those questions. It is common for state's attorneys to act aggressively during their cross examination of the defendant, and your ability to remain calm and collected can carry great weight.

There are a couple things to keep in mind when testifying. Judges and jurors are human beings and the way they see things in the courtroom is similar to the way human beings at large view the world. Judges and jurors will see you throughout the trial so make sure to present yourself throughout the trial the same way you wish to be perceived. That includes dressing appropriately and being respectful to everyone in the courtroom. You should dress no less than what would be appropriate for a church bar-b-que, but suits and ties are favored. Button-up shirts with long sleeves are mandatory. In terms of respecting others in the courtroom, if you are respectful to others while they testify or handle whatever role they play in your case it is more likely the judge or jury will extend you the same respect, but when people act disrespectfully towards others, judges and jurors tend to return the favor when it comes time for them to speak.

Another thing to keep in mind is the fact that judges and jurors are equipped with notepads during trial, and they take notes the same way everyone else does – they start in the top left-hand corner of the page and finish in the bottom right-hand corner. The general flow of your testimony should be to first introduce you to the judge or jury, then bring to the attention to the judge or jury any relationships, names or locations that may come up during your testimony that they may not already be familiar with and then proceeding through the event starting at the beginning and ending with the end of the event.

Starting at the beginning and ending at the end sounds like common sense but it is much harder than it sounds. During trial your attorney is limited to asking you dumb sounding questions like "then what happened" because an attorney is generally not allowed to lead their witness through direct examination. Leading questions sound like "isn't it true that he hit you first" or "isn't it true that he got within inches of your face".

It is imperative that you answer only what is being asked and not ramble through your entire testimony based on one question. By breaking your testimony into smaller parts, you allow your counsel to ask follow-up questions such as "can you explain" or "how far away was he" for portions of the testimony that may need further exploration. If you run through your whole testimony in one shot your attorney will be forced to go backwards repeatedly to clarify and expand on the testimony you just gave, which can make your testimony confusing. We as human beings tend to believe that confusion is indicative of either a witness's failure to recall properly or worse, flat-out deception.

Lastly, judges and jurors, in accordance with the fact that they are human beings, want to feel like they got to know you when you have testified. Make sure to look at the people asking you questions, both your attorney and the state's attorney, and take opportunities to look at the judge and jury as well when you are testifying. Eye contact is one of the limited means by which people can connect in a courtroom where physical touch is disfavored or even illegal. This should not be a robotic process where you are moving your head based on a timer but don't be afraid to look at the people who need to understand you. You have trusted them to decide your case so talk to them and tell them what really happened.

6.0. Concluding words

Here at COHEN | HARRIS LLC, if we had a dollar for every time we've heard someone say Maryland doesn't have a self-defense law, we would be wildly rich. Maryland does have a stringent legal framework under which use of force is judged but that does not mean in any way that you cannot find refuge in its provisions. By understanding what the law requires and working within that framework both during the encounter and subsequently in preparation with your attorney, you can successfully defend yourself, your home, or your property, and ultimately your freedom. It is our wish that no reader of this book needs the information contained within, but the reality is that many of us will face criminals who will claim to be victims and knowing this information can help protect us from unjust outcomes. Although not required by law, it is highly recommended that you obtain an insurance policy that covers legal use of force situations. Companies such as USCCA can be of great assistance should a use of force situation arise.

Roland S. Harris IV, author, and Martin E. Cohen, co-author, can be reached via our office number at 888-585-7979 or email at info@cohenharris.com.

NOTES

NOTES

NOTES

NOTES

NOTES

NOTES

NOTES

NOTES

NOTES

NOTES

NOTES

NOTES

www.ingramcontent.com/pod-product-compliance
Lightning Source LLC
Chambersburg PA
CBHW070349230526
45471CB00006B/2486